BAPTISM OF FIRE
FOR REVIVAL

MICHAEL MARCEL

UKWELLS.ORG

Published by UK Wells.
Website: www.ukwells.org

Table of Contents

Introduction

In my book 'Prepare for Revival', I list four disciplines/ anointings that, in my opinion, we are lacking in the Body of Christ today:

- Holiness
- Travailing Prayer
- Evangelism
- Testimony

I believe these areas are the main reasons why we have not had a revival in England for over one hundred years.

I have taken two of these subjects, Holiness and Travailing Prayer and turned them into booklets because I feel these are vital to our nation. Both booklets point the reader to revival/ evangelism and they are both full of testimonies.

Testimony is really powerful; it brings breakthrough. The word testimony in Hebrew is 'aydooth' which, according to a Hebrew scholar means 'do it again with the same power and authority'. Every time you speak out or read a testimony you are saying to the Lord, 'do it again with the same power and authority'.

I have read several accounts of love-feasts, where Methodist Society members gathered together to worship and give testimonies, that led to revival and cases where revivals have been read out and new revivals have begun. Please remember this as you read these accounts. The language these writers use is not modern English but the stories are still impacting.

My understanding of the Baptism of Fire has developed

since 2005. The more I research this topic, the more my understanding continues to grow.

In this booklet I use the terms Baptism of Fire, Sanctification, Holiness and Christian Perfection. My use of these terms is as follows:

- The Baptism of Fire is a single encounter with God that brings about immediate Holiness.
- Sanctification and Christian Perfection are alternative names for Holiness.

Chapter One

The Revivalists

For many years I have studied the lives of revivalists and there is a common theme in their lives that I have sought to understand. Many of them went from one level of power to another, which took them from being ordinary ministers of the gospel to living as revivalists, with all the signs that follow such a ministry.

It is my belief that they experienced the 'Baptism of Fire'.

> "I baptise you with water for repentance. But after me will come one who is more powerful than I, whose sandals I am not fit to carry. He will baptise you with the Holy Spirit and with fire." (Matthew 3:11)

One hears a lot about water baptism and baptism of Holy Spirit, but very little is preached or written about the 'Baptism of Fire'. The longer people fail to understand the significance of this baptism and therefore fail to live in the benefits of it, the greater the risk that it will be lost forever.

The following are examples of revivalists who have encountered God in a major way, resulting in vastly increased power and anointing. There are more testimonies in the Appendix at the end of the booklet.

A revivalist is someone who promotes or leads a revival or someone who evangelises in a revival atmosphere. Being a revivalist is not an office we hold, it is a role we perform. It is not a role for the few, but for many.

William Clowes

William Clowes co-founded the Primitives Methodists in 1808.

> "..(he) shut himself up in the chamber with the Bible to see what the Lord would do for him. He felt the spirit of burning when he went up; but the Lord gave it to him until it filled every part of his body at once, burning to his finger-ends, and his eyesight seemed for a while to be taken away."[1]

Alexander Macleod

Alexander Macleod ministered in the Hebrides between 1824-1843.

> One day a change took place in his sermons - "They had always been scriptural but commonplace and unarresting sermons, delivered in a pleasant, silvery, easy voice, but now they became tongues of fire that swept into the inner corners of the soul..."[2]

John Harper

> "Four years after being born of the Spirit in 1886, teenager John Harper experienced a baptism of power and an increased passion for souls..."[3]

(see the appendix for the rest of the testimony).

Evan Roberts

Evan Roberts was the most well-known leader of the 1904 Welsh Revival.

"As one and the other prayed I put the question to the Spirit, 'Shall I pray now?' 'Wait a while' said He. When a few more had prayed I felt a living power pervading my bosom. It took my breath away and my legs trembled exceedingly. This living power came stronger and stronger as each one prayed, until I felt it would tear me apart, and as each one finished I would ask, 'May I pray now?' At last, as someone stopped, I prayed. My whole bosom was in turmoil, and if I had not prayed I would have burst. I fell on my knees with my arms over the seat in front of me, my face was bathed in perspiration, and the tears flowed in streams, so that I thought it must be blood gushing forth. For about two minutes it was terrible. I cried out, 'Bend me! Bend us! Oh! Oh! Oh! Oh!' It was God commending His love that bent me. Then the fearful bending of the Judgement Day came to my mind, and I was filled with compassion for those who must bend at the judgement, and I wept. I felt ablaze with a desire to go through the length and breadth of Wales to tell of the Saviour."[4]

W S Jones

W S Jones was a leader of the 1904 Welsh Revival.

"Suddenly there came to me an indelible consciousness of the amazing holiness of God like a purifying fire - like a fiery river flowing out from the throne, and I in the midst as if reclining on it. I do not know whether it were in the body or out of it, but the fire percolated through my whole nature…"[5]

E Keri Evans

E Keri Evans was a leader of the 1904 Welsh Revival.

"…the most I expected was some help to overcome my bad temper…but instead of that I was baptised with streams of life-giving cleansing, transformation power for about half an hour, that made me feel clean and joyous to the depth of my being."[6]

Douglas Brown

Douglas Brown, the leader of the 1921 Fisherman's revival, was happy in Balham. His church was full, he had not known a Sunday in fifteen years without a salvation and he loved his congregation; yet one day in November he returned to the vestry after preaching and broke down. God had started to deal with him, and for four months he wrestled with the Lord. One Saturday night he wrote out his resignation to the church he loved, because he felt that he could no longer preach while he was in contention with God. That night something happened.

"I found myself in the loving embrace of Christ forever and ever; and all power and joy and all blessedness rolled in like a deluge."[7]

Four days later he was in Lowestoft and the revival began immediately.

Duncan Campbell

Duncan Campbell was the leader of the 1949-52 Hebrides Revival.

"After spending seventeen years in a barren wilderness, baffled and frustrated in Christian work and witness, I suddenly came to realise that God had made provision for clean hands and a pure heart. And on my face in my own study at five o'clock in the morning I came to know the recovering power of the blood of Christ... I know that in some small measure - the revival in Skye and later in Lewis, must be related to the experience of that morning. What was it that led me into this full realisation of glorious deliverance in the Holy Ghost? I answer in one word, a baptism from God. Explain it as you will, it was a baptism from God. That experience was in my case preceded by a spiritual hunger, a longing for God to do something."[8]

Duncan Campbell clearly believed that what happened to him was Sanctification (clean hands and a pure heart); although the others do not put it in this way, I believe that is what they received as well.

You can see from the varied descriptions above that there is no set manifestation regarding receiving the Baptism of Fire. You may feel fire or you may not.

Chapter Two

Biblical Context

Apart from Matthew 3:11 and Luke 3:16 (which are identical verses), what does the Bible say about the Baptism of Fire?

Fire is mentioned in several contexts in the Bible, but in this case the fire is like that explained in Malachi 3:2.

> *"For He is like a refiner's fire and like launderers' soap."*

Those who are Baptised with Fire are purged, refined, the consequences of sin in their life is dealt with, the pollution that sin leaves in our lives is removed and the demonic is removed. It is a life changing experience.

As you receive Sanctification the dross in your life is burned up, and as a consequence you are able to access more of the power of God, which is seen in the lives of the Revivalists mentioned earlier.

> *"Now to Him who is able to do exceedingly abundantly above all that we ask or think, according to the power that works in us."* (Ephesians 3:20)

If we are refined through the Baptism of Fire, we will be like gold, which becomes a better conductor, as more impurities are taken out.

Isaiah 6:1-8 explains the process.

In the year that King Uzziah died, I saw the Lord sitting on a throne, high and lifted up, and the train of His robe filled the temple. Above it stood seraphim; each one had six wings: with two he covered his face, with two he covered his feet, and with two he flew. And one cried to another and said:

"Holy, holy, holy is the LORD of hosts; The whole earth is full of His glory!"

And the posts of the door were shaken by the voice of him who cried out, and the house was filled with smoke.

So I said: "Woe is me, for I am undone! Because I am a man of unclean lips, And I dwell in the midst of a people of unclean lips; For my eyes have seen the King, The LORD of hosts."

Then one of the seraphim flew to me, having in his hand a live coal which he had taken with the tongs from the altar. And he touched my mouth with it, and said:

"Behold, this has touched your lips; Your iniquity is taken away, and your sin purged."

Also I heard the voice of the Lord, saying: "Whom shall I send, And who will go for Us?"

Then I said, "Here am I! Send me."

Remember the Seraphim are 'fire' angels. After this experience Isaiah was sanctified and as a consequence God was able to use him in a greater way. What you see here is a commissioning as a consequence of Sanctification, which is what I believe happened to all the revivalists mentioned above.

John the Baptist says that after refining there is a connection to bringing in the harvest - in other words 'revival'.

> *"His winnowing fan is in His hand, and He will thoroughly clean out His threshing floor, and gather the wheat into His barn; but the chaff He will burn with unquenchable fire."* (Luke 3:17)

I believe that the revivalists quoted above have all experienced the Baptism of Fire. Having been refined, they received from Holy Spirit much greater authority and power to bring in a harvest of souls.

There are also a few difficulties with some verses in the Bible. In Acts 1:5, Jesus says the disciples would be baptised with Holy Spirit, but does not mention 'fire'. The fact that 'fire' came when they were in the upper room leads me to think that as far as Jesus was concerned 'fire' was included when receiving 'Holy Spirit'. The same applies to similar verses in Acts 10 and 11 when Cornelius and his household are baptised.

Chapter Three

Where has the Baptism of Fire gone?

We have seen precious little of the Baptism of Fire since 1900; it was there in Biblical times, so what has happened to it?

I believe that John is talking in Luke 3:16 and Matthew 3:11 about two separate parts of the same baptism, one of the Holy Spirit and one of 'fire'. I also believe that these two baptisms are meant to be experienced together, as the disciples experienced them in the upper room in Acts 2, when they were visited by the wind and the fire.

Things changed in the fourth and fifth centuries, when people stopped believing in the Gifts of Holy Spirit and they started to believe that Holy Spirit was only for New Testament times (something that is still taught in some churches today). It amazes me that people stopped seeing miracles, signs and wonders only a few hundred years after Jesus' ministry.

Thinking about why this happened, I have concluded that Christians continue to have the same problem generation after generation: they simply do not believe what the Bible says.

Up to the time of the Reformation, they had some excuse because very few people had access to a Bible, but we have no such excuse today. If someone does not get a revelation from the Bible on a subject, then it will not be taught, and Biblical truth will disappear from the Church, even though there may be a small remnant with the knowledge.

If people do not testify to what they experience, others will have no idea what the Bible offers and that it is available today.

The first person I have traced who had that revelation was John Wesley. He did not call it the Baptism of Fire, and I am not sure if he connected the two; he called it Sanctification or Christian Perfection. He yearned for the blessing of Sanctification.

In 1771, he wrote the following in a letter to the Countess of Huntingdon,

> "Many years since, I saw that *'without holiness no man shall see the Lord.'* (Hebrews 12:14) I began following after it, and ten years later, God gave me a clearer view than I had before of the way how to attain this, namely, by faith in the Son of God."

In 1738, Wesley was the first man to preach that Sanctification and Salvation could be received by faith.

I have to admit that for years I ignored Hebrews 12:14 because it was too challenging for me, but now I realise how important it is. The full verse in the Passion Translation says,

> *"In every relationship be swift to choose peace over competition, and run swiftly toward holiness, for those who are not holy will not see the Lord."* TPT

In the Notes of the Passion Translation, the Aramaic can be translated as *"no man will see into the Lord."*

The more we embrace Holiness the closer we will get to God. The closer we get to God, the less of our sinful mindset exists and more of Him will be seen in us. This transformation allows God to use us in greater ways.

The importance that John Wesley placed on Holiness can be

seen by the system of Classes and Bands that he set up within his Societies, across every area of the country. These were the precursors to the home groups that exist today. They were the engine rooms of the Methodist movement and you would only be invited to join one if you were considered to be a passionate Christian.

On Christmas Day 1738, Wesley set out the rules for these Classes.

> "The design of our meeting is, to obey that command of God, 'Confess your faults one to another, and pray one for another, that ye may be healed…'" They met once a week and started with singing or prayer and then, "To speak each of us in order, freely and plainly, the true state of our souls, with the faults we have committed in thought, word, or deed, and the temptations we have felt, since our last meeting."

These Classes were bodies of holy people, in close relationship with one another, chasing after God, wanting to go from glory to glory. Small wonder that God blessed the Methodist movement with so many revivals. In my thirty-one years of being a Christian I have never heard of any home group doing this.

There were signs of Sanctification in the days of the Great Awakening,

> "After preaching I talked with M.B., who has been long 'a mother in Israel.' 'I was under strong convictions,' she said, 'when twelve or thirteen years old, and soon after found peace with God. But I lost it by degrees, and then contented myself with living a quiet, harmless life, till Mr. Charles Wesley came to Wednesbury, in the year 1742. Soon after this my convictions returned, though not with terror, as before, but with strong hope; and, in a little time, I

recovered peace and joy in believing. This I never lost since, but for forty-eight hours (by speaking angrily to my child). Not long after, Mr. Jones talked particularly with me, about the wickedness of my heart. I went home in great trouble, which did not cease, till one day, sitting in my house, I heard a voice say, in my inmost soul, 'Be ye holy; for I am holy.'

From that hour, for a year and a quarter, (though I never lost my peace,) I did nothing, but long, and weep, and pray, for inward holiness. I was then sitting one day, August 23, 1744, about eight in the morning, musing and praying as usual, when I seemed to hear a loud voice, saying at once to my heart and to my outward ears, 'This day shall salvation come to this house.' I ran upstairs, and presently the power of God came upon me, so that I shook all over like a leaf. Then a voice said, 'This day is salvation come to this house.' At the instant I felt an entire change. I was full of love, and full of God. I had the witness in myself, that he had made an end of sin, and taken my whole heart forever. And from that moment I have never lost the witness, nor felt anything in my heart but pure love."[9]

In 1741 John Wesley spoke on Sanctification or what he called Christian Perfection. He said,

"Ye are 'perfect men' being grown up to the measure of the stature of the fullness of Christ... It is these only are properly Christians."[10]

The idea that you could not be a proper Christian without receiving Sanctification was controversial and something he clarified at their 1746 Conference.

"Sanctification to denote the gradual death to sin and growth in grace begun at justification; and the particular use of the term "Entire Sanctification" to denote that instantaneous total death to sin and entire renewal in the love and image of God achieved through faith which enabled the Christian to rejoice evermore, to pray without ceasing, and in everything to give thanks."[11]

In 1758 Wesley wrote that Christian Perfection was:

"Loving God with all the heart, so that every evil temper is destroyed, and every thought, and word, and work springs from and is conducted to the end by the pure love of God and our neighbour."[12]

John Wesley's expectations regarding a Holiness revival finally became manifest in their fullness in the 1760 Otley Revival. He had received the following letter from Otley, Yorkshire:

"On Friday, February 13th, about thirty persons were met together at Otley, about eight o'clock in the evening, in order (as usual) to pray, and sing hymns, and provoke one another to love and good works. After prayer was ended, when they proceeded to speak of the several states of their souls, some, with deep sighs and groans, complained of the burden they felt for the remains of in-dwelling sin; seeing in a clearer light than ever before, the necessity of a deliverance from it.

When they had spent the usual time together, a few went to their own houses; but the rest remained upon their knees, groaning for the fulfilment of the great and precious promises of God. One being desired to pray, he no sooner began to lift up his voice to God, then the Holy Ghost made intercession in all that were present, with groanings that could not be uttered. At length the travail of their souls burst out into loud and ardent cries. They had no doubt of the favour of God, but they could not rest, while there was anything in them contrary to His nature. One cried out, in an exceeding great agony, 'Lord deliver me from my sinful nature!' Then a second, a third, and fourth. And while the person who prayed first was calling upon God in these words, 'Thou God of Abraham, Isaac, and Jacob, hear us for the sake of thy Son Jesus!' one was heard to say, 'Blessed be the Lord God for ever, for He hath cleansed my heart.' Another and another spoke the like experience, and the writer thus concludes: thus they continued for the space of two hours; some praising and magnifying God, some crying to Him for pardon or purity of heart, with the greatest agony of spirit.

The next evening they met again; and the Lord was again present to heal the broken in heart. One received remission of sins; and three more believed God had cleansed them from all sin. And it is observable; these are all poor, illiterate creatures, of all others most incapable of counterfeiting, and most unlikely to attempt it. But 'when his word goes forth, it gives light and understanding to the simple.'"[13]

The huge importance this news meant to Wesley can be seen by how quickly he visited the Otley area. Clearly, he had already planned a trip to Ireland, but after speaking in nine towns on the way, he diverted from Stockport to Leeds. He had a terrible journey across the moors and spent the next day interviewing people. Then the following day he rode through a dreadful storm back over the Pennines, to continue his journey to Ireland.

He wrote, in his Journal on the 12th March,

"I spent the greatest part of this day in examining them one by one. The testimony of some I could not receive; but concerning the far greatest part, it is plain (unless they could be supposed to tell wilful and deliberate lies)

(1) that they feel no inward sin, and to the best of their knowledge commit no outward sin;

(2) that they see and love God every moment, and pray, rejoice, give thanks evermore;

(3) that they have constantly as clear a witness from God of Sanctification as they have of justification. Now in this I do rejoice, and will rejoice, call it what you please; and I would to God thousands had experienced thus much, let them afterward experience much more as God pleases."

Alexander Mather, a Methodist minister at Darlaston, West Midlands, describes how he felt when he was Sanctified.

"What I had experienced in my own soul was an instantaneous deliverance from all those wrong tempers and affections which I had long and sensibly groaned under; an entire disengagement from every creature, with an entire devotedness to God: and from that moment, I found an unspeakable pleasure in doing the will of God in all things. I had also a power to do it, and the constant approbation both of my own conscience and of God. I had simplicity of heart, and a single eye to God, at all times and in all places; with such a fervent zeal for the glory of God and the good of souls, as swallowed up every other care and consideration. Above all, I had uninterrupted communion with God, whether sleeping or waking. O that it were with me, as when the candle of the Lord thus shone upon my head! While I call it to mind, my soul begins to wing its way toward that immediate enjoyment of God. May it never be retarded, but press into the glorious liberty, which is equally free for all the sons of God."[14]

John Wesley considered Otley the most important revival of his life; it was the deepest, most far-reaching, and the most lasting. He thought of it as the Methodist Pentecost and compared it to the revival that launched the Church in Jerusalem. He summarised it as follows:

"During the whole time many have been convinced of sin, many justified, and many backsliders healed. But the peculiar work of this season has been what St Paul calls 'the perfecting of the saints'. Many persons in London, in Bristol, in Yorkshire, and in various parts both of England and Ireland, have experienced so deep and universal a change as it had not before entered into their hearts to conceive. After a deep conviction of inbred sin, of their total fall from God, they have been so filled with faith and love (and generally in a moment) that sin vanished, and they found from that time no pride, anger, desire, or unbelief. They could rejoice evermore, pray without ceasing, and in everything give thanks. Now, whether we call this the destruction or suspension of sin, it is a glorious work of God - such a work as, considering both the depth and extent of it we never saw in these kingdoms before."[15]

Chapter Four

John Wesley's Sanctification

The whole idea of Sanctification was really important to John Wesley, but when people said they had received it, he did not just get excited that he had been proven correct, he spent a lot of time checking people out to make sure that they were not fooling themselves or him. He was well aware that there were people who would copy what they saw happening to others (as they do today) and he was also aware that some people claimed that they received Sanctification only to see them fall back into their old ways several weeks later. He was very analytical; I think he would have made a good scientist!

When he first came across it at the time of the Great Awakening; he and another man interviewed people who claimed to have received it to see if what they were claiming was genuine. Also, during the Otley revival he did much the same thing. He came up with three reasonable proofs that someone had been sanctified.

(1) If we had clear evidence of his exemplary behaviour for some time before this supposed change. This would give us reason to believe he would not 'lie for God,' but speak neither more nor less than he felt.
(2) If he gave a distinct account of the time and manner wherein the change was wrought, with sound speech that could not be reproved.
(3) If it appeared that all his subsequent words and

actions were holy and unblamable."[16]

Also, "None therefore ought to believe that the work was done, till there is added the testimony of the Spirit witnessing his entire Sanctification as clearly as his justification."[17]

A classic testimony was recorded by Wesley in his Journal in March 1760. The lady, who wanted to remain anonymous is referred to as MS. She said,

"I was born April 8, 1736. My father died when I was between four and five; my mother, when I was about eleven years old. I had little thought about religion, and seldom so much as went to church. But I had even then many troubles, which made me sometimes think of God, and cry to him for help. When I was about seventeen, I was asked one Sunday to go and see a pit, which was on fire and blazed out. It was near the house where Mr. James Jones was then preaching. I was standing near the house, when my brother persuaded me to go in: I liked what I heard; but it was above a year before I knew myself to be a lost sinner. For three weeks I was in deep distress, which made me cry to God day and night. I had comfort once or twice, but I checked it, being afraid of deceiving myself; till, as Mr. Johnson was preaching one morning at five o'clock, in Darlaston, my soul was so filled with the love of God, that I had much ado to help crying out. I could only say, 'Why me, Lord; why me?'

When I came home I was exceeding weak, having also a great pain in my head: But all was sweet: I did not wish it to be otherwise. I was happy in God all the day long; and so I was for several days. From this time I never committed any known sin, nor ever lost the love of God; though I found abundance of temptations, and many severe struggles. Yet I was more than conqueror over all, and found them easier and easier. (Proof 1)

About Christmas, 1758, I was deeply convinced there was a greater salvation than I had attained. The more I saw of this, and the more I prayed for it, the happier I was. And my desires and hopes were continually increasing for above a year.

On January 30, 1760, Mr Fugill talked with one who thought she had received that blessing. As she spoke, my heart burned within me, and my desire was enlarged beyond expression. I said to him, 'O Sir, when shall I be able to say as she says?' He answered, 'Perhaps tonight.' I said, 'Nay, I am not earnest enough.' He replied, 'That thought may keep you from it.' I felt God was able and willing to give it then and was unspeakably happy. In the evening, as he was preaching, my heart was full, and more and more so, till I could contain no more. I wanted only to be alone, that I might pour out my soul before God; and when I came home I could do nothing but praise and give him thanks. (Proof 2)

From that moment I have felt nothing but love in my heart; no sin of any kind. And I trust I shall never any more offend God. I never find any cloud between God and me: I walk in the light continually. I do 'rejoice ever more,' and 'pray without ceasing.' I have no desire but to do and suffer the will of God: I aim at nothing but to please him. I am careful for nothing, but in all things make my requests known to him with thanksgiving. And I have a continual witness in myself, that whatever I do, I do it to his glory." (Proof 3)

I am grateful to Charles H Goodwin, who, in his booklet 'The

Methodist Pentecost', compared this testimony to the three proofs that Wesley was looking for. He writes,

> "The first proof required of the sanctified person was a genuine experience of justification expressed in a changed life successful in conquering sin. The testimony of MS begins, therefore with an account of her awakening to her need for pardon, and her experience of justification."

Wesley wrote that inward Sanctification begins,

> "In the moment we are justified. The seed of every virtue is then sown in the soul. From that time the believer gradually dies to sin and grows in grace."[18]

He also wrote,

> "A Christian is so far perfect as not to commit sin. This is the glorious privilege for every Christian, yea, though he be but a babe in Christ."[19]

> "Yet, sin remains in him; yea, the seed of all sin, till he is sanctified throughout"[20]

Despite the obvious need for Sanctification and the numerous examples of people receiving it, Wesley found great difficulty in trying to persuade his ministers to teach it. They seem to have been in agreement that people need to work out their Sanctification, growing into it gradually, but against the idea of receiving it instantaneously.

J W Laycock writes about one leading minister's reticence,

> "To this work at Otley William Grimshaw alludes in his letter to C. Wesley, March 31st, 1760. He evidently thought that 'sinless perfection' was being taught and professed, and from this and other letters

we gather that Grimshaw's views on this 'perfection' were felt by himself to be not quite in harmony with what he looked upon as Methodist teaching on this experience.

He says 'The doctrine of perfection runs very high, just now, in these parts. About Otley and Leeds, I am told, not fewer than thirty profess sinless perfection; and thirty more, I expect, will pretend there to shortly. If it be of God, it is well. Time will prove it. I wish they knew their own hearts. My perfection is, to see my own imperfection; my comfort, to feel that I have the world, flesh, and devil to overthrow through the Spirit and merits of my dear Saviour; and my desire and hope is, to love God with all my heart, mind, soul, and strength, to the last gasp of my life. This is my perfection. I know no other, excepting to lay down my life and my sword together.'"[21]

Wesley believed that putting the hope of instant Sanctification to the people would incentivise them to pursue it. He wrote,

"The constant experience shows the more earnestly they expect this, the more swiftly and steadily does the gradual work of God go on in their soul; the more watchful they are against all sin, the more careful to grow in grace, the more zealous of good works, and the more punctual in their attendance on all the ordinances of God. Whereas the contrary effects are observed whenever this expectation ceases... Destroy this hope, and that salvation stands still or, rather, decreases daily."[22]

By 1772 John Wesley declared that his preachers might believe in Christian Perfection, but never preached it. Charles Goodwin conjectures that the failure of Wesley to win his people over may have been because of the controversy concerning his earlier teaching that you were not a proper

Christian until you have received Sanctification. Even though Wesley tried to clarify that he did not mean that you needed Sanctification to get into heaven; this may have been a stumbling block for his ministers. The people were happy with the teaching of Justification by faith; they did not wish to labour after anything else.

Having said that, I have read the biographies of around forty of Wesley's itinerant preachers and many of them give testimony of their desire for and eventual receiving of instant Sanctification. This could come in a relatively few weeks or after a few years of searching. Here are two examples.

Robert Lomas writes,

"Saturday (in June) before private prayer in the forenoon, I was led to think much about my indifference, unfaithfulness, and wanderings, and the causes of these things; I concluded that my heart was not so much devoted to God and his work as it ought to be, and that I wanted a great salvation. For some years I had seen the possibility and necessity of entire Sanctification; and that it was the work of God, and obtained by faith, and therefore might be granted in one moment. Now these things rested with uncommon weight upon my mind, and I was much drawn out to pray that the Lord would cleanse me from sin. I cried to the Lord with many tears and strong wrestlings, Oh! Lord. I beseech thee, deliver my soul. It was not long before my soul felt a calm, and a sinking before God, conscious that He must do the work, or it must be undone: then my faith grew stronger, and my soul waited for His salvation. In a very little time I could rejoice in God with joy unspeakable and full of glory. I knew, I felt that He had entire possession of my heart, and that He was all my own. I found unspeakable pleasure in repeating the words of the Psalmist, 'I am thine, I am thine,

thine!' I am thine! I cried again and again, and my soul was filled with rapture, Glory be to God for his mercy!"[23]

Richard Rodda writes,

"The doctrine of Christian perfection was now preached among us, and numbers professed they had attained the blessing. I had not the least doubt of the testimony of several, as their whole behaviour agreed with their profession. I believed the doctrine, and my soul longed to experience it. I prayed that every thought and desire might centre in God. While my eldest brother and I were pouring out our souls to God for this blessing, the Lord poured out His Spirit upon us; every heart present appeared like melting wax before the fire; and in that hour, God gave my mother a testimony that He had cleansed her from all unrighteousness; which I trust she retains to this day.

My soul was now on full stretch after the blessing. I not only believed it attainable, but that I should attain it: therefore I constantly expected that Christ would come to cleanse and keep my heart. Accordingly, one Saturday night, I came to the class, and resolved not to depart till mine eyes had seen this great salvation. After I had entered the room, my heart seemed as hard as a stone; but I was not discouraged. All my prayer was, 'Lord, create in me a clean heart, and renew in me a right spirit.' The mighty power of God descended upon me; my heart was emptied of every evil, and Jesus took up all the room. I could no longer refrain from telling what God had done for my soul. My heart was filled with love and joy, and my lips praised Him."[24]

A common theme of testimonies I have read is their doubts. Each one had an amazing encounter with the Lord when they received Salvation and again when they received Sanctification, yet doubts flooded their minds that they had not actually received what they had been searching for or that they had lost it. It just shows that when we have an extraordinary encounter the enemy may try to snatch away the blessing. We must always be watchful and stand firm. A similar situation is often experienced by people who have received a healing - unless one stands on it the enemy can put doubts in one's mind and you can lose it.

Wesley also believed that Sanctification was crucial for the spreading of revival. He wrote,

> "Wherever the work of Sanctification increased, the whole work of God increased in all its branches."[25]

In 1762 he wrote.

> "Where Christian Perfection is not strongly and clearly enforced, the believers grow dead and cold."[26]

Are we like that today?

In 1766 he wrote,

> "Where Christian Perfection is not strongly and explicitly preached, there is seldom any remarkable blessing from God, and consequently, little addition to the Society, and little life in the members of it... Till you press the believers to expect full salvation now, you must not look for any revival"[27]

This is the root of why I believe that the Baptism of Fire/ Holiness is so crucial for revival. The less sin in us, the more Holy Spirit can operate in us, and the more God can use us; the more God pours out through us the more revivals there will be.

Chapter Five

Sanctification after John Wesley

The teaching of Sanctification died out in the United Kingdom until after John Wesley's death, however he managed to export it to America. He sent three great men to America. Thomas Rankin, Francis Asbury and Richard Whatcoat, were all believers in Wesley's teaching on Sanctification. They led several Holiness revivals in America from 1784 to 1792 and some sixty thousand were added to the Methodist church.

The teaching of Holiness went into decline for a while, but then Phoebe Palmer and her sister began to promote it in meetings in their homes in 1835 and the great Holiness revival movement began in America.

After Wesley's death in 1791, Holiness teaching began to appear again in England through the likes of William Bramwell and the founders of Primitive Methodism, William Clowes and Hugh Bourne.

Here are two testimonies from that period:

"I (William Bramwell) was for some time deeply convinced of my need of purity and sought it carefully with tears and entreaties and sacrifice; thinking nothing too much to give up, nothing too much to do or suffer, if I might attain this pearl of great price. Yet I found it not, nor knew the reason why until the Lord showed me I had erred in the way of seeking it. I did not seek it by faith alone, but as it were, by the works of the law. Being now convinced of my error, I sought the blessing by faith alone... When in the house of a friend... I was sitting... with my mind engaged in various meditations concerning my affairs and future prospects, my heart now and then lifted up to God, but not particularly about this blessing, heaven came down to earth; it came to my soul. The Lord, for whom I had waited, came suddenly to the temple of my heart; and I had an immediate evidence that this was the blessing that I had for some time been seeking. My soul was then all wonder, love and praise. It is now about 26 years ago; I have walked in this liberty ever since."[28]

"Mr. George Smith was that year (1807) stationed at Ashby de la Zouch and had heard wonderful things about the revival at Sheffield. Having been long in search of the blessing of Sanctification, he resolved to go to the place where it was reported many others had received it... Messrs. Bramwell, Pipe, Longden, and Miller, were present: and while they and other able witnesses gave a clear and Scriptural account of the manner in which they received the gift of Sanctification, the strangers (Mr. George Smith and his friends,) were much affected. Mr. Miller exhorted all the faithful to lift up their hearts in behalf of these earnest and sincere seekers. They began to pray for them; when Mr. Smith was so overwhelmed with the power of the HIGHEST, as instantly to enter into the sanctifying rest, which remains for the people of God.

Constant communion with God the Father and the Son fills their hearts with humble love. Now this is what I mean by perfection. And this I believe many have attained, on the same evidence that I believe many are justified."[29]

James Caughey came over from America in 1841 and had very successful meetings with many Salvations and many received Sanctification, including William Booth (founder of the Salvation Army). He was followed by Phoebe Palmer in 1859 who stayed in the United Kingdom for several years. William and Catherine Booth really took over the mantle of Holiness teaching until the end of the century.

William Booth's interest in Holiness increased after a conference was held on the subject to which church leaders came from all over the country. This was led by William Boardman, an American revivalist. When the War Cry began in 1879, Booth put a Holiness article in it every week for at least three years. Around the same time there were Holiness meetings all over the different Salvation Army Corps. They were about receiving the Baptism of Fire and I have read in 'The Salvationist' and 'The War Cry' many accounts of people saying that the Holiness meeting was vital for the work of evangelism. Those who received this Baptism, received more of God's power and a greater passion for the lost. Booth placed it in the forefront of his teaching wherever he went, it was a major key to the success of the Salvation Army.

In April 1869, someone wrote about why it was so important - we really need this today:

> "This is what we are crying for in the East of London. The baptism of the Holy Ghost, and of Fire. But how much more might be done had you all received this Pentecostal baptism in all its fulness. If every soul were inflamed, and every lip touched, and every mind illuminated, and every heart purified with the hallowed flame. O what zeal, what self-denial, what meekness, what boldness, what holiness, what love would there not be? And with all this, what power for your great work? The whole city would feel it. God's people in every direction would catch the fire, and sinners would fall on every side. Difficulties would

vanish, devils be conquered, infidels believe, and the glory of God be displayed.''

A Holiness meeting was held every week at Headquarters, and they were very powerful:

> William's son, Bramwell Booth comments were reported in the Christian Mission magazine. "He was entirely convinced, that something of the same force which manifested itself on the day of Pentecost manifested itself at those meetings in London. He describes how men and women would suddenly fall flat upon the ground and remain in a swoon or trance for many hours, rising at last so transformed by joy that they could do nothing but shout and sing in an ecstasy of bliss... He saw bad men and women stricken suddenly with an overmastering despair, flinging up their arms, uttering the most terrible cries, and falling backward as if dead supernaturally convinced of their sinful condition. The floor would sometimes be crowded with men and women smitten down by a sense of overwhelming spiritual reality, and the workers of the Mission would lift their fallen bodies and carry them to other rooms, so that the Meetings might continue without distraction. Doctors were often present at these gatherings. Conversions took place in great numbers; the evangelists of the Mission derived strength and inspiration for their difficult work, and the opposition of the world only deepened the feeling of the more enthusiastic that God was powerfully working in their midst."

The following article from The Christian Mission Magazine for September 1878, gives an account (edited) of "A Night of Prayer," lasting from August 8th-9th:

> "The whole company, amounting to three or four hundred, settled down for the whole night, a very

great advantage over meetings from which many
have had to retire at midnight or early morning and
from the beginning to the end, weary as almost everyone was, after four days of almost ceaseless services,
the interest and life of the meeting never diminished.

Scarcely had the first hymn been commenced, when
a company of butchers assembled in a yard next
door, with the avowed intention of disturbing us,
commenced a hullabaloo with blowing a horn, rattling
of cans, and other articles, so as to keep up a ceaseless
din, which was heard even whilst the whole company
sang aloud. But nobody was disturbed. We felt we
were fighting, that was all, and everyone seemed to
sing all the more gladly and confidently, Glory, glory,
Jesus saves me, Glory, glory to the Lamb.

The great object of the meeting was to address God,
and it was in prayer and in receiving answers that the
meeting was above all distinguished.

Evangelists came there burdened with the
consciousness of past failings and unfaithfulness
and were so filled with the power of God that they
literally danced for joy. Brethren and sisters who
had hesitated as to yielding themselves to go forth
anywhere to preach Jesus, came and were set free
from every doubt and fear, and numbers whose
peculiar afflictions and difficulties God alone can
read came and washed and made them white in the
Blood of the Lamb.

That scene of wrestling prayer and triumphing faith
no one who saw it can ever forget. We saw one collier
labouring with his fists upon the floor and in the air,
just as he was accustomed to struggle with the rock
in his daily toil until at length he gained the diamond
he was seeking; perfect deliverance from the carnal

mind, and rose up shouting and almost leaping for joy. Big men, as well as women, fell to the ground, lay there for some time as if dead, overwhelmed with the Power from on High. When the gladness of all God's mighty deliverance burst upon some, they laughed as well as cried for joy, and some of the younger evangelists might have been seen, like lads at play, locked in one another's arms and rolling each other over on the floor.

God wrought there with a mighty hand and with an outstretched arm, so as to confound the wicked one and to raise many of His people into such righteousness and peace and joy in the Holy Ghost as they never had before, and thousands, if not millions, of souls will have to rejoice forever over blessings received by them through the instrumentality of those who were sanctified or quickened between the 8th and 9th of August, 1878.

The usual un-intoxicating wine not having been prepared for sacrament, we managed uncommonly well with water, and in fact everybody seemed to have got into a condition in which outward circumstances are scarcely noticed, and the soul feasts on God, no matter what passes outside. Under Captain Cadman's energetic leading eightyone bore their clear simple testimony to the Blood that cleanses from all sin in a very few minutes over that time, and after a little prayer we parted."

A month later, Ballington Booth (William and Catherine's son), gives a brief (edited) description of a "Holiness Meeting," which is interesting:

September 13th was a wonderful time. Never shall I forget it. Oh, God did search all hearts that night.

After speaking about giving up all and being kept by the power of God, and singing 'I am trusting, Lord, in Thee,' we fell on our faces for silent prayer. Then God Almighty began to convict and strive. Some began to weep, some groaned, some cried out aloud to God.

One man said, 'If I cannot get this blessing I cannot live'; another said, 'There's something, there's something. Oh, my God, my God, help me. Set me straight; put my heart straight.'

Many more were smitten. Five or six more came forward. One dear man took his pipe from his pocket and laid it on the table, resolved that it should stand between his soul and God no longer. Then six or seven more came forward. Everyone was overpowered by the Spirit. One young man, after struggling and wrestling for nearly an hour, shouted 'Glory! glory! glory! I've got it. Oh! Bless God!' One young woman shook her head, saying, 'No, not tonight,' but soon was seen on the ground pleading mightily with God. Every un-sanctified man or woman felt indescribably. Three or four times we cleared the tables and (penitent) forms, and again and again they were filled.

So we sang, cried, laughed, shouted, and twentythree had given their all to the Master, trusting Him to keep them from sinning, as He had pardoned their sins.

Never can I forget Tuesday night's Holiness Meeting, held in the Salvation Chapel, Spring Garden Lane... God backed the speaking with convicting, cutting power, after which His Spirit was poured upon us in an overwhelming manner. Immediately afterwards some twenty rushed forward for this freedom from sin. Weeping and groaning commenced in all parts, when some twenty more rushed forward. Oh, the scene at this juncture. One dear lad, not above seventeen, after lying his length on the ground for some time, cried out, 'Oh, it's come. I have it. Oh, God! my God! my God! You do cleanse me.' Then followed more wrestling and agonising, and the forms again being cleared of those who had obtained liberty.... Once more we cleared them, but only to make room for more who were waiting to come out but at this point nothing could be heard save sobs and groans and heart-rending prayers. Thus continued this mighty outpour until upwards of seventy rose testifying with feelings indescribable and unutterable joy, while all around stood weeping and rejoicing, singing and shouting.

After prevailing prayer Captains Smith, Haywood, and Coombs gave powerful testimonies of Christ's taking away and keeping from the desire of sin. I felt unutterably filled with the Spirit. Never shall I forget the scene that took place when all unsanctified were asked to come forward. It seemed as if Christ said, 'What will ye that I should do unto you?' There was a cry on all sides. Some fifteen or sixteen rushed to the front. After this, over twenty more rushed forward; while those who had obtained the blissful peace stood round singing, with faces of rapture and tears of joy." More idols cast at Christ's feet; more rose feeling the liberty; more room was made for those yet seeking; more rushed forward; and while weeping and wrestling and groaning on all sides. Some nine or ten forms were cleared until over two hundred came forward seeking in an agony of soul and heart a life of purity. We finished this meeting with 250 testimonies.

A few people carried the teaching on through the first half of the twentieth century, but today there is hardly any sign in the

United Kingdom of the Holiness Movement.

In my years as a Christian I have hardly ever heard Holiness preached and through my research I have concluded that the mainstream teaching of Sanctification in the United Kingdom has been virtually non-existent for the last seventy years.

However, I believe that now is the time for instant Sanctification - the Baptism of Fire - to be received again.

Baptism of Fire

I love this saying from Smith Wigglesworth,

> "Repeat in your heart often, 'baptised with the Holy Ghost and fire, fire, fire!'
>
> All the unction, and weeping, and travailing comes through the Baptism of Fire, and I say to you and say to myself, purged and cleansed and filled with renewed spiritual power."[30]

Bob Jones was one of the most accurate prophets in the world, and he had some truly staggering words, some of which were to do with the formation and growth of the International House of Prayer in Kansas City. In the 1970's he died and went to heaven, but God told him to go back to prepare for the billion soul Revival He was planning, which he would see the beginning of before he died.

Bob announced the beginning of the Revival in November 2013 and he died on Valentine's Day 2014. Every year he would give a prophesy for the year ahead and his last one, which is on his website says:

> "Bob was handed a huge white egg and as it was placed in his hand it began to hatch open. As he drew closer to examine the egg, he saw that it had fire inside and it was like a birthing of fire.
>
> This egg represents a new birthing and new life because it represents the second birthing of the baptism of fire. This baptism will be far greater than Pentecost and more powerful than Azusa Street of

recent times. I believe we're all getting ready to be birthed a second time in fire. This was the timing and we will see the fire of God this year.

It's the same kind of fire as the burning bush that was not consumed. I believe that now is a time of commissioning like when Moses received his instructions. When this egg opens, the wisdom that will be given is that of the Father's will because it will reveal the Father's heart to us. Then our only testing will be obedience to that which the Father puts in our conscience.

This Baptism of Fire means that plagues and viruses cannot cling to it. No demonic control can survive around it and the enemy cannot trouble you. The Baptism of Fire will bring in holiness and holiness is one of the main words this year. God is a holy God and when we are consumed by this baptism of fire, anything unholy that comes into our presence will not be able to stand. The power of this consuming fire will cause demons to flee and sickness, disease, infirmities and plagues to die instantly. There will be no question that the power of God is resident in His people."[31]

Up until six years ago I had only heard the subject spoken of once or twice in many years. Now suddenly a number of people are giving talks on the subject; it really seems to be a subject on God's Heart. This is not surprising, as the Baptism of Fire is likely to be a precursor to Revival and Revival in the United Kingdom is expected soon.

How do we receive it?

a. By Faith

According to John Wesley, just as we are Justified by faith, so

are we Sanctified by faith. If we know our Kingdom identity -
who we are in Christ - and pursue a relationship with God, we
can receive it by faith, but we have to appropriate it and apply
it. There is a cost, a cost of time. I do not think it a coincidence
that many of the revivalists I have researched and who had
received the Baptism of Fire, spent something like three hours
a day with the Lord. It did not matter that they would probably
be ministering in the evening; they still spent hours with God,
because that is where their strength and power came from.

> "McKendrick was a tireless labourer and through
> the years made no fewer than sixteen trips to the
> Isle of Lewis, six journeys to Shetland and countless
> visits to villages, towns and cities all over Scotland
> and England. In 1909 he relocated to Australia,
> where, relentlessly, he held missions throughout that
> vast land. Speaking honestly, yet without egotism,
> towards the end of his earthly labours, the evangelist
> shared what must help explain his amazing ministry
> of genuine anointing:

> 'I have preached on an average 450 times a year for
> the last 28 years. Yet I can truly say I have spent
> more time upon my knees alone before God than
> I have spent on the platform before men. Fine talk
> and eloquence in preaching are not always power
> - indeed, such gifts are oft times a hindrance and a
> snare and prevent true dependence upon God. A
> prayerless man must be a powerless man; a prayerful
> man is a powerful man... It is this that makes life
> worth living"[32]

W P Nicholson, a Northern Irish revivalist in the 1920s, also
considered prayer vital.

> "The secret of his power was no doubt in his prayer
> life. He stayed at our home for ten days during the
> campaign, and although he was up in the morning

at six o'clock, he never appeared until twelve noon. He spent the hours wrestling with God in prayer. My wife would take up his breakfast and leave it outside his bedroom door, but it was rarely taken in. By his own special request he was not disturbed by phone or visitor, however urgent."[33]

I am sure that the revivalists of today do the same. I remember the Canadian revivalist, Todd Bentley saying several times that he would spend at least three hours a day before the Lord. I am not saying that to get the Baptism of Fire we need to spend three hours daily with the Lord - but it helps!

We need to be hungry and spend time seeking Him. As a consequence of our hunger and our change in lifestyle, there is more of Him and less of us, which leads to us receiving more power and authority. It is all about the presence of God in our lives.

John Wesley's sermons, books and essays about Christian Perfection can be found on the internet. Another important work on receiving Sanctification by faith is, 'The Higher Christian Life', by William Boardman, published in 1858 (it can be read online at archive.org). This was an extraordinarily popular and influential book. Boardman had been desperate to receive Sanctification, so he tried everything he could to receive the blessing, however nothing worked. After six months he realised, like William Bramwell, that you could not receive it by 'works', so he gave up everything and trusted in Jesus. Boardman then received Sanctification and preached on the subject for years at conferences all over America. He came to live in London in 1876 and apart from teaching on Holiness, he was probably the first person to teach on and practice healing. Someone close to him wrote of him after his death, "The love of God was the very atmosphere which he breathed, and it shone in heaven's light upon his face." Would we all not want this said of us? Clearly, Boardman, after receiving Sanctification, kept the benefit for the rest of his life.

b. Impartation

We can also receive the Baptism of Fire through impartation. Some people are carriers of it - Sergio Scataglini for instance. Sergio was one of the young leaders in the Argentine revival who had a revelation of Holiness. He had a significant encounter with the Lord and then preached on Holiness throughout the world.

In his book, 'The Fire of His Holiness'[34], Sergio reported that God had said '98% holiness is not enough', and he used the analogy, would you buy a bottle of water that said 98% pure water and 2% sewage?[35]

I was in one of Sergio Scataglini's meetings about fifteen years ago and I know that I received an impartation of Holiness through him. There were no physical manifestations, but when I got home I was changed.

c. Sovereign Encounter

The third way to receive the Baptism of Fire is through a Sovereign encounter, which is how Wesley's leaders received it and what Bob Jones and others have prophesied. I want to suggest that He brings a measure of Holiness through His presence; in other words, from the outside - in. Although, He could be activating more of the Holy Spirit that is already within us - or both.

My friend received it this way. She was in Israel several years ago when a travelling companion beckoned her to come into a church they were visiting, saying that she thought God had something for her there.

> "I was very tired and grumpy and suddenly the power of God hit me. It was like I had been plugged into electric sockets and I was really scared, I could feel His presence but the Holiness and the Fire that was

pouring through me cascaded down, over me and in me and through me, and it went on and on and on and I shook and shook and shook. These Christians I was travelling with took hold of me and they said 'you are receiving the Baptism of Fire.' That manifestation continued. I began to worship God with what sounded like Aramaic and Hebrew sounding tongues, over and over and over, I was filled with the love of God, absolutely filled with the love of God and that was a demarcation time in my life, I completely changed at that point.

What was placed into me was an empowerment to live in holiness. What happened to me was that Baptism of Fire took out of me the desire to sin. I have lived in that manifestation ever since, I do not have the desire to sin. The temptation is not in me, that does not mean I walk perfectly, but from that point there was a complete change in my life and there was a purity that I was given by the infilling of the Baptism of Fire.

I came back from Israel and for days and days and days afterwards I just continued, I was absolutely full of the love and the purity and the holiness of God. I had no fear; I was given God's love for people at a different level and a passion for His Presence again was at a different level. He began to heal me. The Spirit of Fire inside of me was just cleansing me, purging and healing me. I came out of a lot of brokenness; a lot of abuse and I was different."

We must encounter the Lord, align with His purposes and pull down the Baptism of Fire. We are in partnership with God; He makes it available and we have to pull it down from heaven onto the earth in prayer. Clearly the Lord is making the Baptism of Fire available at this time, so we now need to ask for the Baptism of Fire and for Revival. We must also make it known to the Body of Christ so that they can pull it down as well.

I should point out that some of you reading this will say that you have already experienced Sanctification/Baptism of Fire. I believe some people experienced this when they were saved or when they received the Baptism of Holy Spirit, but did not recognise this at the time.

While waiting to receive the Baptism of Fire it is important to seek after Holiness. Just as Justification is an ongoing work, Sanctification is also an ongoing process. For many sanctification/holiness will come from the gradual renewing of the mind, rather than a sudden encounter with God.

> *"Do not conform any longer to the pattern of this world, but be transformed by the renewing of your mind."* (Romans 12:2)

Part of this journey might be to remove the roots from inside through Christian counselling and deliverance ministry. For example, you might have control issues, the root of which is embedded in childhood experiences or teenage rejection.

I puzzle about why, in my experience, Holiness is taught so little in Church. Is it because there is a cost involved and pastors are afraid of preaching it because it is not populist teaching? Whatever the reason, Christians tend to pay little attention to it, although this is nothing new. William Bramwell wrote in 1807:

> "I am certain there is much more religion among us than any other body in England; and yet the preaching of Sanctification, and living in it, are much in decline. How this is to be remedied I cannot tell. It must end in something bad if this glory cannot be restored."[35]

You can see how important it was to Bramwell.

Today's consumer society is one that is not conducive to people seeking Holiness. Many, mistakenly, think that they are holy because they go to church, or read their Bible a little, or pray at times. An example of what I mean can be seen regarding healing. I believe that there are so many sick Christians because we have got out of the habit of seeking God for our healing; instead, our first stop is a doctor.

Another blockage within the Body of Christ is Hyper-grace. Hyper-grace teaches that God forgives one's future sins the same way he forgives one's past sins. Some even say that repentance and confession of sin are not necessary since Christians are eternally forgiven. Those who think that way obviously will feel there is no need for Holiness teaching because they think that they are always holy, despite evidence to the contrary. This is a very dangerous view that must be removed from the Church.

There is also the old excuse that everyone is too busy to seek Holiness, but we must do everything we can to make time! God tells us many times in the Bible to be holy. Here are just two:

> *"Who may ascend the hill of the LORD? Who may stand in his holy place? He who has clean hands and a pure heart, who does not lift up his soul to an idol or swear by what is false. He will receive blessing from the LORD and vindication from God his Saviour."*
> (Psalms 24:3-5)

> *"But just as he who called you is holy, so be holy in all you do; for it is written: 'Be holy, because I am holy.'"* (1 Peter 1:15-16)

Why would the Bible tell us so often to be holy if it was not important to God? If it is so important to God should it not be equally important to each of us?

Why would people in the world want to be part of a Church which is full of Christians who are just as immoral and sinful as they are? Clearly, the answer is they do not. We are meant to be in the world, but not of it. We need to be set apart through Holiness. It is no coincidence that Methodists of the eighteenth and nineteenth centuries considered Holiness vital in a Christian's character, and they moved in great power and saw a great many revivals and awakenings as a result.

The fact is that the Church has, in recent decades, become more and more like the world and this has got to change and change quickly. We need to pursue a new Holiness move in the Body of Christ. I believe that the teaching of Sanctification generally stopped at the end of the 19th Century and I do not think it a coincidence that it is virtually 100 years since we had an Awakening in England.

Interestingly, the last revival in the United Kingdom was in the Hebrides (1949-52) and Holiness played an important part. Before the revival began some people prayed in a barn for six weeks until a young man declared that the prayers were wasted unless they were right with God.

> "Then he lifted his two hands and prayed, 'God, are my hands clean? Is my heart pure?' But he got no further. That young man fell to his knees and then fell in a trance onto the floor of the barn. In the words of the minister, at that moment, he and his other office bearers were gripped by the conviction that a God sent revival must always be related to Holiness, must ever be related to Godliness. Are my hands clean? Is my heart pure?
>
> When that happened in the barn, the power of God swept into the parish and an awareness of God gripped the community such as hadn't been known for years. And on the following day the looms were silent, little work was done on the farms as men and women gave

themselves to thinking on eternal things, gripped by eternal realities."[36]

I hope that by recounting the experiences above I have been able to persuade you that the Baptism of Fire is available to you and that Holiness is absolutely key to revival - it is up to you and me to help bring it back into the Body of Christ.

Appendix

Additional Testimonies

John Macdonald

John Macdonald was an incredible revivalist who ministered in the beautiful, but often bleak, north of Scotland and the Hebrides around 1800.

"But he passed through a still more important change during his residence in Edinburgh. There is no record of his experience at that time, but of his having made a fresh start in the way of life there was abundant evidence. There have been instances of renewed men becoming 'other men' under a fresh baptism of the Spirit. This was the change which Mr. Macdonald underwent in Edinburgh. It was soon apparent in his preaching. Always clear and sound in his statements of objective truth, his preaching now became instinct with life; it was now searching and fervent, as well as sound and lucid. Knowing the terror of the Lord, as he knew it not before, he warned sinners in Zion with such faithfulness and power as excited the wonder and the awe of his hearers. His statements of gospel truth were now the warm utterances of one who deeply felt its power. The Lord's people could now testify that he spoke from his own heart to theirs. So marked was the change which then passed over his preaching, that many were led to judge that he had never preached the gospel till then."[37]

John Harper

"Four years after being born of the Spirit in 1886, teenager John Harper experienced a baptism of power and an increased passion for souls. The next day he took his stand on a street in his native village of Houston, Renfrewshire, and strongly entreated all in his audience to become reconciled to God. Impressed by his obvious gifting, the Pioneer Mission supported him in forming a church in 1897 with twenty-five members.

Growth came quickly, and a corrugated iron hall was built at Kinning Park dockyards in 1901, seating 550. While a born expositor, Harper was preeminently an evangelist whose entire ministry was soaked in prayer. When he spoke, 'the words came hissing hot from his heart... he lived and preached as if Christ died yesterday, rose today, and was coming tomorrow.' One colleague spoke of 'constant revivals' in Harper's church, with overflowing crowds and hundreds of souls saved and blessed. The most memorable season of blessing was in 1905, being preceded by many months of earnest and united prayer for such occasion."[38]

Joseph Jenkins

Joseph Jenkins was a leader of the 1904 Welsh Revival.

"He refused to lose his grip on His Lord until He had blessed him, and indeed he was blessed for he was clothed with strength from above, and he knew it. And then, when he rose from his knees a strange blue flame took hold of him until he was almost completely covered. It rose, as far as he could gather, from the floor of the room and billowed up, encircling him..."[39]

Jock Troup

Jock Troup was an ordinary preacher, but something happened that made him a revivalist.

> "Mrs Troup has reminded me that the secret of all her husband's ministry was the mighty experience that took place in 1920 in the Fisherman's Mission at Aberdeen. Something glorious happened there that made him the man he became. He entered into a definite experience with the blessed Holy Spirit. This experience was so sacred to him that he did not mention it often, and then only to a few intimate friends. I am sure our beloved brother would have called it 'a baptism of power for service'. In Bible conferences and revival rallies I have heard him again and again emphasise his belief that every Christian must have a definite dealing with the Holy Spirit for an effective witness for Christ."[40]

The following year he was in Great Yarmouth, where he experienced the revival which had spread from Lowestoft and then he took it back to many parts of Scotland.

James Turner

This man was an evangelist for years and after several months of searching wrote;

> March 4.1854 - My soul is longing to enjoy the blessing of Perfect Love. Dear Mr. Mason says, God will give it soon. Why not today? It is to be got by simple faith. I know what faith is, I have faith, but I have not this faith.

> March 6. - This day, by the grace of God, I can say the blood of Jesus has cleansed my soul from all sin. On Sunday night about 10 o'clock, in my dear

Sister R's house, I was enabled to lay hold, by simple faith, of my dear Jesus. When the Lord converted my soul more than 13 years ago, the Rev. Yule was the instrument in God's hand of awakening me. But on the morning that I got pardon and peace, there was no man with me, nor had I any help but, what the Holy Ghost afforded. But in getting into perfect love, the Lord made use of two dear Sisters (M. R. and J. W.) full of God indeed, and dear to my heart. They had to lift poor me into God. How He gave them power to bear me up on the arms of faith, and when the power of God came down on me, it sunk me to the floor speechless, and then I lay for some time full of the glory of God, and I feel it until this hour. Satan has done what he can to take the blessing from me, but I am sweetly resting on Jesus — all is well. He is mine and I am His. He has put the white robe on me. This moment He is feeding me with the hidden manna; His kisses are sweet to my mouth.

During the 1860 awakening James Turner led an estimated 8,000 to the Lord in the Moray Firth area of Scotland.

End Notes

1.   Memoirs of the Life and Labours of the Late Venerable Hugh Bourne: By a Member of the Bourne Family published 1854, page 106.

2.   Banner in the West, by John Macleod, published by Birlinn, page 146.

3.   Glory in the Glen, by Tom Lennie, published by Christian Focus, page 102-3.4. Lives of Early Methodist Preachers, by Thomas Jackson, Volume 6, page 65.

4.   http://www.revival-library.org/pensketches/ revivalists/testrobertse.html

5.   Living Echoes of the Welsh Revival 1904-05 by Robert Ellis, Chapter 7. From the cd 'Welsh Revival Library'.

6.   My Spiritual Pilgrimage by Keri Evans, published by James Clarke 1961, page 63.

7.   A Forgotten Revival, by Stanley C Griffin, page 18, published by Day One Publications.

8.   The Price and Power of Revival, sermon by Duncan Campbell.

9.   Wesley's Journal, April 16th, 1757, Dudley.

10.   The Limits of Love Divine, by W S Gunter, page 104.

11.   The Limits of Love Divine, by W S Gunter, page 104.

12.   The Life and Times of John Wesley, Volume II, by L Tyerman, page 307.

13.   Wesley's Journal, March 17th, 1760.

14.   The Early Methodist Preachers, by Thomas Jackson, Volume 2, page 189.

15.   Wesley's Journal, November 15th, 1763.

16.   A Plain Account of Christian Perfection, by John Wesley, page 48.

17.   A Plain Account of Christian Perfection, by John Wesley, page 52.

18.   The Works of the Rev John Wesley, Volume 4, page 356.

19.   A Plain Account of Christian Perfection, by John Wesley, page 19.

20.   A Plain Account of Christian Perfection, by John Wesley, Chapter 5.

21.   Methodist Heroes in the Great Haworth Round 1734-1784, by J W Laycock, 1909, page 203-4.

22   The Works of John Wesley, Volume 4, page 403.

23   History of Wesleyan Methodism in Halifax and its neighbourhood. By J U Walker, page 189-90.

24   The Lives of the Early Methodist Preachers, Volume 2, by Thomas Jackson, page 303.

25   The Works of John Wesley, AM: Letters, page 314.

26   The Works of John Wesley, Volume 3, page 91.

27   John Wesley's Letter to George Merryweather, February 1766.

28   Memoir of the life and ministry of William Bramwell, by William Bramwell and his family, published in 1848, page 36-7.

29   A Chronological History of the People called Methodists, by William Myles, 1803, page 72.

30   A Life Ablaze with the Power of God, by Smith Wiggles worth, page 3.

31   http://bobjones.org/index.cfm?zone=/Docs/Words%20 of%202013/2013-10_BaptismOfFire.htm

32   McKendrick, page 259-60.

33   A statement by A Lindsay Glegg in All for Jesus, the Life of W P Nicholson, by Stanley Barnes, page 129.

34   The Fire of His Holiness, by Sergio Scataglini, published by Renew Books in 1999, page 35.

35   Memoir of the life and ministry of William Bramwell, by William Bramwell and his family, published in 1848, page 223.

36   A taped recording of a Duncan Campbell sermon in 1968.

37   The Apostle of the North by John Kennedy, page 28, published originally in 1866, reprinted in 1978.

38   'Glory in the Glen,' by Tom Lennie published by Christian Focus Publications, p102-3.

39   Cyfrol Goffa, pages 36-37.

40   Our Beloved Jock, by James Alexander Stewart.

41   'James Turner or How to Reach the Masses' by E McHardie, page 9.

MICHAEL MARCEL'S OTHER BOOKS

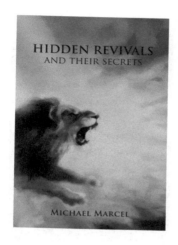

This book records the nine most significant revivals/awakenings that took place in the United Kingdom over the last 400 years. It is very important to know the exciting stories of the amazing things God has done in the UK that is part of our spiritual heritage.

We can be set on fire by reading the stories and wonderful testimonies of people who experienced the power of God. They will excite you and give you a vision of how to light fires of revival in your area!

This book is available through www.ukwells.org

MICHAEL MARCEL'S OTHER BOOKS

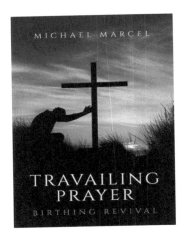

"There really is an anointing on this book and my spirit gets so stirred as I read. I find myself "eating" the content more than reading it. I deeply connect with this. You have built a beautiful case for the power and fruit of travailing prayer. It is very comprehensive in it's descriptions and content.

Karen

This book is available through www.ukwells.org

MICHAEL MARCEL'S OTHER BOOKS

"Michael Marcel has made himself a student of Revival. His thorough approach to any task, coupled with his passion for Jesus, make this a great resource for anyone seeking and praying for revival. Revival remains the cry of my heart, a cry which was ignited in a Pastor's House where every Friday night I attended a prayer meeting for Revival, just after I was saved in 1973. It is stirred again as I read. This book will prompt you to prepare and pray for Revival."

Paul Manwaring
Director Global Legacy & Deployment,
Bethel Church Redding, CA.

This book is available through www.ukwells.org

MICHAEL MARCEL'S OTHER BOOKS

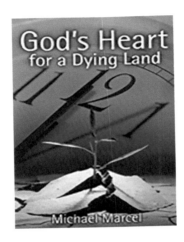

'God's Heart for a Dying Land', is a passionate cry from the heart of one who yearns to see the Church take its rightful position in today's society. It is rich in history and would be an invaluable resource for anyone who has a burden for the nation and who wants to translate that into prayer that brings about lasting change.

Agu Irukwu
Senior Pastor
Jesus House for all Nations (RCCG)

This book is available through www.ukwells.org

MICHAEL MARCEL'S OTHER BOOKS

"In this book Michael raises questions and offers some solutions for the future reformation of the church; including the need for people to turn their faces and gifts towards our society so that it can be changed. You will find this book a worthwhile challenge."

Dr Sharon Stone
Founder and Apostle
Christian International Europe

This book is available through www.ukwells.org

.

BV - #0048 - 160524 - C0 - 216/138/3 - PB - 9781908154415 - Matt Lamination